MAN CAVE

A ONE-MAN SCI-FI CLIMATE-CHANGE TRAGICOMEDY

(ANNOTATED)

by Timothy Mooney

MAN CAVE

A ONE-MAN SCI-FI CLIMATE-CHANGE TRAGICOMEDY

(ANNOTATED)

by Timothy Mooney

MAN CAVE

Credits:
Cover Illustration by David C. Jensen
Cover Photos by Tisse Mallon
Photo Compilation by Marcus Fernando

ISBN 13: **978-0-9831812-7-9**
ISBN 10: **0-983-1812-7-6**
LCCN: **XXXXXXXXX**

ABOUT THE AUTHOR:

Timothy Mooney has adapted seventeen of Molière's plays into rhyming English verse, seen in the United States and around the world, many of them published by Playscripts and Stage Rights. He recently expanded into the work of Carlo Goldoni with a rhymed version of *The Servant of Two Masters*. Tim's one-man plays, *Molière than Thou, Lot o' Shakespeare, Breakneck Hamlet, Breakneck Julius Caesar* and *Shakespeare's Histories; Ten Epic Plays at a Breakneck Pace!* are turning a new generation on to Molière and Shakespeare, while Mooney's *The Greatest Speech of All Time* brings to life actual historical speeches spanning from Socrates through Martin Luther King. Tim is currently working on *Thy Will*, a play about the "Shakespeare Authorship" question.

Previously, Tim taught acting at Northern Illinois University and published his own newsletter, *The Script Review*. As Artistic Director of the Stage Two Theatre, Tim produced nearly fifty plays in five years. Inaugurating the *TMRT Press* in 2011 with his long-awaited acting text, *Acting at the Speed of Life; Conquering Theatrical Style*, Tim followed up with *The Big Book of Molière Monologues* before publishing parts of his one-man catalogue, including *Molière Than Thou, Criteria, a One-Man Comic Sci-Fi Thriller!, Shakespeare's Histories; Ten Epic Plays at a Breakneck Pace!, Breakneck Hamlet* and *Breakneck Julius Caesar*!

DEDICATION:

To the courageous work of Guy R. McPherson, leading authority on climate change leading to near-term human extinction, and author of the blog, "Nature Bats Last."

Also, to the work of Dan Kinch, Artistic Director of Brooklyn Culture Jammers, and author/performer of "Planet Hospice," which inspired this play.

SPECIAL THANKS:

To the folks who show up in living rooms to lend me their ears when all this stuff is in its early incubation. Also special thanks to my favorite artist, David C. Jensen who created our cover illustration.

Thanks, also, to the many contributors who made this new show, and our new not-for-profit venture, the Timothy Mooney Repertory Theatre, possible, as well as those who contributed directly to this project, listed on the reverse side of this page.

Donors to the
"Help Bring Man Cave to the Final Frontier" Campaign

Allan Brown
Anonymous (6)
Donna Craig
Jack Dixon
Polly Esther
Pat Hall
Julie Higginbotham
Ted Jekiel
Terry Hall
Andrea Holliday
Larry Kirwan
Mark Long
Mallory
Timothy J. Mooney
Sandra Palombi

Thanks also to our "Planetary Ambassadors," who helped to spread the word: Shawn Murphy, Mallory Sabetodos Vance, Aliki Marie Pantas Semones, Jeff Glass, Madeline Franklin, Polly Esther, Carol Alleman, James Fisher, Gale Pergande, Jack Dixon, Winnie Wenglewick, Emil Guillermo, Donna Craig, Taylor Martin, Jennifer Irle, Daniel Sparks, and others.

The **Help Bring Man Cave to the Final Frontier Campaign** can still use your support. If this is a program you would like to see out in the world, your donations to the Timothy Mooney Repertory Theatre (a 501(c)3 Not-for-Profit organization) would be welcomed at:

Timothy Mooney Repertory Theatre
P.O. Box 638
Prospect Heights, IL 60070

Note: *The "TMRT Press," while sharing goals and vision (and Tim Mooney) is not affiliated with the Timothy Mooney Repertory Theatre and this book (which touches more directly on political themes), is* ***not*** *a not-for-profit effort.*

Table of Contents

From the Author iii

Cast of Characters vii

Production Notes ix

Man Cave 7

Post-show Discussion/Commentary/Exegisis 31

From the Author...

> WARNING: This introduction (as well as much of the "Discussion/ Commentary/Exegesis) contains "spoilers," as I work to make sense of how the material in the beginning of this play connects with stuff in the end, and vice versa. I tend to repeat my discussion of some of these things here and there, but when I find myself encountering an interesting theme, I like to acknowledge it each time it appears, as it appears. I work from the baseline assumption that 90% of those who might pick up this book have already some exposure to the issues of abrupt climate change and possible near-term human extinction. If not, it's probably best to skip ahead to the script now, before coming back to this, or peeking at the end pages.

With that said...

All of the "reasonable people" on TV these days are insisting that we had really better do something about climate change sometime within the next fifty years, or BOY, WILL WE BE IN TROUBLE!

Their arguments are "balanced" by the very "unreasonable people" who go on the TV machine to insist that the whole thing is a hoax and will never affect us in any way, no-how... or if it did, well, there was certainly nothing we puny humans could do about it.

Splitting the difference between fifty years and infinity is still, pretty much... infinity. Imagine a see-saw, with one person straddling the middle of the balancing board, and another person sitting all the way to the right side of the board.

More to the point, as James Temple puts it,[1] "Various politicians, fossil-fuel interest groups and commentators have seized on the uncertainty inherent in climate models as reasons to doubt the dangers of climate change, or to argue against strong policies and mitigation responses."

---

1 Technology Review, December 6, 2017, "Global Warming's Worst-Case Projections Look Increasingly Likely"

A media that gives equal time to the "reasonable people" and the "unreasonable people" (lining up on one side of the argument) will always end up tipping the argument in the direction of the unreasonable, at least as long as those unreasonable people are always on the same side of the argument.

Anybody who tries to come to a reasonable ***conclusion*** from those voices on the TV, will most likely find themselves inspired ***not-in-the-least*** to take action in the near-term, and remain unperturbed by a congress or a president that, for instance, withdraws from the Paris accords and, instead of taking action, ***eases*** restrictions on coal/gas/oil corporate interests.

Which means that any possibility of finding balance in this argument means that we really need some ***unreasonable*** voices at the ***opposite*** end of this equation, flooding the airwaves with the urgency of a calamity that will appear far more suddenly than we have ever allowed ourselves to imagine.

Only by preparing for a disaster that is ready to strike TOMORROW (actually, today, if we've been paying any attention), can we hope to cope even with the most conservative of 50-100 year estimates. And if it so happens that the calamity should continue to expand and magnify at an exponential rate, it will be "game over" long before we currently imagine.

With that in mind, this science fiction tragicomedy is not necessarily an exaggeration. Some of the facts and figures have been rounded in one direction or another, if only to ease the accessibility of the information necessary to grasp the epic size of the pending disaster. The greatest uncertainty that surrounds these facts and figures lies in the particular way they may interact with each other, and the yet-unknown dynamic of the "feedback loop" which may outpace our expectations of the coming disaster far faster than we currently anticipate.

Seeing and hearing all of these details in one place in the course of 50 minutes may, perhaps, bump a percentage of the audience into some greater semblance of action.

Or, not.

All of these things are "true," in the sense that I am citing contributing factors which will interact with each other to crank-up the calamity. I am describing them in relatively unscientific language, if only to startle us into "ACKNOWLEDGING SCREAMINGLY IMPOSSIBLE IMPROBABILITIES."

I'm not a scientist. I'm a dramatist. And an actor. If I listed out only the micro-analyzed details of every last thing that could be asserted with assurance, you would be asleep before realizing that ***this shit is going down***.

But here's what you ought to know: my assessment of this science fictional future is nowhere near the sudden race toward disaster that some scientists (who understand this far better than I do) have been predicting. While I may suggest at some point in this play that the date of the ultimate disaster is X years away, there are extremely knowledgeable people in this community who will assert that the actual date is more likely ***one-tenth*** X into the future.

And, as fatalistic as this play may seem, even I cannot bring myself to accept such a wildly accelerated schedule, if only due to the fact that long before this book ever might reach publication, there would be no one left to buy or read books, or to attend plays.

So, if you're reading this now: smile! You've dodged the bullet (thus far).

But, in other words, ***my own self-interests*** prevent me from seeing this issue with dispassionate scientific realism. I am candy-coating this because that is the only path that I can currently imagine which might lead to success for this project.

And of course, it is that very self-interest which is the biggest issue confronting the society that this play implies.

Normally, I write these one-man plays that I do, and perform them myself, and drive them around the country, scraping together whatever kind of a living that I might, usually as the only guy performing them … for years on end.

I'm not interested in cornering the market this time around. This message is too crucial this time, and one man playing to audiences of twenty or so at a time will not tip the scale to such a degree to alter the path that we're currently taking. What is needed is to get a small army of actors, say, some 50 performing in all 50 states, or hundreds across the world.

So… if you're an actor, reading this right now… maybe envision yourself in the lead role as you contemplate the future.

Tim Mooney, 2018

Cast of Character

Tim, an affable personality, who just happens to find himself or herself locked away in a "Hobbit Home" of sorts.[2]

Time: The Near Future.

Place: Northern Canada

[2] Obviously "Tim" is a name I chose for (I assume) obvious reasons: I wanted to strip away any barrier between myself and the character, and identify with this character as fully as possible. I would anticipate that any future performers of this material will feel free to insert their own names in place of "Tim." Also, there is no real reason why the performer might not be female, rather than male.

Production Notes

The performance text is followed by a rather elaborate Discussion/ Commentary/Exegesis beginning on page 31. I realize that numerous references may be abstract, surprising or dubious to the casual student or reader, and I'd love for you to have the full contextual background to understand, or to explore for yourself and develop your own conclusions about this increasingly urgent threat to our survival.

In staging this piece, we used only a few props: A small table, such as a card table, or perhaps a round table, big enough to hold a microphone and a laptop computer. One of the visual inspirations that I sometimes contemplate are the famous "Dogs Playing Poker" paintings, which usually feature a series of various dogs in comic poses around a green felt-topped table, with an overhead lamp emphasizing the isolation of the figures at the table.

It's not necessary to have an actual lamp suspended above the table. In fact, you may want to "cheat" the implied beam of light so that when "Tim" gets up and walks around the table, he won't disappear entirely into the blackness.

We discovered that the chair that "Tim" sits at works best as one of those swiveling desk chairs, which can pivot smoothly, allowing an easy rise to the left or the right, without bumping into the table legs.

"Tim's" costume should be the sort of thing that s/he would wear around the house on a relatively hot day when 100% confident that no visitors are going to show up. For my opening performances, I chose the always-amusing checkered boxer shorts, in coordination with a red "Flash" t-shirt. There's something about the lightning "Flash" symbol that suggests both the speed and the vengeance of nature... even, perhaps of the lingering desire to race backwards through time.

We also littered the table with a small handful of post-it notes, to give "Tim" the occasional external impulse for his occasional jump to a seemingly unrelated subject matter (as he finds himself reminded of some perspective he had thought-up the night before).

I'm largely going to stop adding quotes to "Tim" from this point forward (only using them in spots where there might otherwise be confusion). You can assume, unless noted otherwise, that Tim refers to the character, not "me.

Man Cave

A One-Man Sci-Fi Climate Change Tragicomedy

(Annotated)

The Play

And

Discussion
Commentary
Exegesis

BLACKOUT

TIM (*In Blackout*)
"Greetings, Earthlings."

LIGHTS UP.
Tim, at microphone, patched into his laptop at a small table.

TIM
Just kidding. Had to get that one out of my system.

Actually, I have no idea if there even are any earthlings still out there.

I mean, I'm pretty sure there's somebody, but, you know, "within the sound of my voice" is an open question.

But, for that matter, we've been sending these signals out into the universe[3] for, what? A hundred years? No idea if, or where they land. Maybe, as I speak now, you're watching re-runs of the Honeymooners. Or, well, they won't be re-runs where you are. "Bang. Zoom. To the moon, Alice!"

No, really, we're not all like that. And, even that was intended to be a parody of the whole *patriarchal* thing.

We're not monsters.

---

[3] I realize the process of underlining may be distracting at first, but it's the simplest way I can think of to alert you to the availability of a corresponding note in the "Post-Show Discussion." It is not meant to indicate any extra-special stress coming from Tim's delivery. (I save *italics*, **bold** and UPPER CASE for that.)

Sometimes we're worse.

So, for what it's worth, I'm broadcasting from north. Fairly far north. Northern Canada north… about as far north as you can get without being in the actual Arctic Circle. I don't know if there's anybody else up here who managed to dig in before it all became unlivable. Anywhere south of here is too hot to survive. Anywhere north is just about pure methane gas. So, I managed to burrow into a hillside, load up on Campbell's soup and air filtration units and seal the door.

So. I'm here now. No going back out.

But, hey, there's wi-fi. And a radio tower.

Internet's been pretty quiet these days, though. I keep hitting "refresh."

But you know, if you're out there, I'm Tim@Tmail.com[4].

I inherited that address from somebody who doesn't seem to be using it anymore.

Sometimes I send myself emails, just to hear the little "ding!" Make sure it all still works.

I'm trying to figure out how to rig the internet to recognize any changes in whatever remote corner of it might still be working. Maybe a Google alert…? Set to, like, every possible word?

Internet? I don't know how it is you're still out there. Are you in the cloud somewhere?

Hey: refresh.

[4] Obviously, any equivalent ridiculously simple email address (that is not being used as someone's actual email address) can be substituted for your turn at this role.

Ack! Damn Huffington Post. I remember when you'd have something new up every five minutes. Now I'm stuck with ugly Ted Cruz[5], again and again and again for eternity. Enough to make you want to claw your eyes out.

CNN and USA Today are worse. Gohmert and Inhoffe. Flat Earthers.

Mars colony 1; are you out there? Anything? A ding? Hello?

Was going to have a Mars Colony 2, 3, 4, and on up… Never quite relocated Cape Canaveral in time.

But hey, we did manage to send off Nina Mission 1 before it all fell apart. You guys out there? Was supposed to be a Pinta and a Santa Maria too.

I know, you're moving. Too fast for my voice to catch up. Approaching speed of light yet? Passing Pluto?

You know, there's nobody here to contradict me, so I hereby declare it a planet again. I don't care what that fucking Neil Degrasse Tyson says. [6]

Yeah, I know. He was right on all the other shit.

So, here I am… all alone in my cozy little hobbit home. No Gandalf heading my way to muck up the door. No one to talk to: no one answering the email "ding"… At first I thought it was temporary, until a really bad August blew over. Even way up here, we were looking at daytime temps of 120. (Fahrenheit! Not Celsi-uhh… Centigr-- I still can't get used to that shit.)

No, I'm not Canadian. Wish I was; I wouldn't feel so… culpable.

Night-time was cooling off to a breezy hundred-and-five.

---

[5] If the naming of actual politicians is too divisive for your audiences, you may substitute fictional political villains. Though I would suggest that the mockery of actual climate deniers goes a long way to shaming them out of their evil ways.

[6] Of course, any epithet describing Neil Degrasse Tyson may be substituted here. But "fucking" really does seem to get a good laugh, if only because he's such a congenial fellow to begin with, we know that this angry remark is actually about something deeper going on within the character of Tim.

You know, these temps aren't unheard of. Usta be, you'd have a hot spell for a week or so. Sometimes, people dying of heat exhaustion. Someplace like Chicago, might be 20, 30 people.

Actually, ***now*** that would be a really, really good day. When it all went world-wide, a good day might be 20, 30 thousand.

Even then we had the idiot Libertarians[7]: "Thin the herd!" "Survival of the fittest!"

They pretty much turned out to be not among the fittest. But who knows? Maybe one of 'em is in a bunker somewhere… "Rand Paul?"

No, that's right. Rand Paul was in D.C. when that place lit up like a tinderbox. Of course, it's possible that some of them are still twenty stories below, where they keep all the good Kentucky bourbon.

I didn't load up on booze until it was too late. (*Picking up his coffee cup, half filled with water*) At least I've got water… my own pump, my own well… I've also got one of those crazy filtration units that turns pee back into water… (*choosing to return his cup to the table rather than take a sip*) saving that for last resort. Like when the pump goes dry, or water gets contaminated. I don't know if the water or the air conditioning will go first. The air is powered by solar, but the main unit is outside… shaded by - solar panels… But once that goes?

> (*TIM stands, walks around his chair or the table, mostly throwing his voice toward the microphone.*)

Oh, right. August. Was up to 120. September? Around 110. October-November? Maybe 100-*ish*. It's not really going "back down."

So, here we are... or, here I am, anyway… Nothing to do but talk into the void. Why stay? Why not let go?

---

[7] We don't actually have to call the Libertarians "idiots" if that's an issue. And Tim isn't actually calling all Libertarians "idiots." What he means is, "All the libertarians who are ignorant and heartless enough to think that dumping vast populations as if they were excess baggage is an effective survival strategy. "Damn Libertarians" or just simply "all the Libertarians" will work just as effectively.

Good question. Maybe my answer sounds ridiculous. But it's the only one I've got.

(*TIM sits, on "humanity experiment."*)

You see, I'm not entirely certain this whole humanity experiment was ever actually ***supposed*** to work. Sure, we managed to develop opposable thumbs, generate cognitive thought, create the wheel and tools, and the internet and Shakespeare… not in that exact order.

You know how a baby is, like, universally loved?

Even the really ugly ones have something in them that sets off a… a *nurturing genetic code,* turns us all into puddles of smiling and cooing and gibberish. Which is great.

And at the other end of that, those babies are getting hugged and cuddled and fed and changed. And that's great too.

Except that that baby assumes that that phase is going to last. Because that baby assumes that all of that love and cuddling and food is probably something that they ***deserve***.

Meanwhile, we all learned to outsmart the animals that wanted to kill us, we bent the land and the elements to do our work for us: to feed us, to light and heat our homes, to cool our cars, to protect us from intruders… We were smart. We kept ourselves safe… But for those of us who stayed safe over time, we mostly decided that that was something that we ***deserved***. The world was cuddling and cooing and feeding us… sometimes providing us with… more intimate pleasures.

And we were good with that! How great that we deserved all that. We must have done something really special to be so really loved. God must really love us to give us all that.

Hm.

You know, I hope there's a God. That would be nice.

Maybe I'm the last one to go, and they're all calling out, "Come join us, come join us…!"

(*Pause, looking around…*)

Not hearing that right now.

(*TIM stands, walks around.*)

But the human impulse is like that baby impulse. Before long you're walking and talking, and they stop loving you for who you ***are***, but for what you can ***do***. And that's kind of a shock, when you realize that you're the one who's ultimately responsible for your own shit. And, as a baby, you're in for some down days… some down years… well into adolescence where you finally get the concept of "your own shit," and you learn not to lie in it, but to clean it up. (That's, um… both literal and psychological shit.)

So the evolving species is like that baby who just won't grow up. Despite what we learn from math and science… we're still looking for that parent figure - that "God," if you will - to clean it up. And because we hate the idea of cleaning it all up, we project words into God's mouth:

God says, "How arrogant of you, you puny humans, to think that you can possibly damage the beautiful planet that I gave you with your pitiful technology?"

"I gave you food, water, sky… coal, gas, oil, fusion, fission… to have dominion over! To use, and enjoy! You ungrateful bastard. Driving a Prius."

(*TIM sits.*)

And I guess it's pretty much the same for that baby: You have been cooking me food. You are the lord of the stove, and I am not worthy to touch it. You have dominion over the lawn and the vacuum cleaner, and it is not for me to touch, or to improve, or to damage.

We give away our responsibility for management of the thing, when *that thing* is so vast and incomprehensible that we could never collectively wrap our heads around it.

And if we ever DO manage to wrap our heads around it, it's usually bad news. Much easier to say, "I am not ***meant*** to understand, but rather to ***accept*** this generous bounty."

Of course, there are always those nay-saying infidels who insist that carbon has built up to over 500... no ***600*** parts-per-million, and certain death will ensue unless we radically change our behavior.

It's really actually much easier to give up smoking. And sex. And eating.

Oh, right, "the big why."

Look, we're about done here. My air hasn't broken down. My water hasn't dried out. But tomorrow may be another question. Or the day after that, or the day after that. When summer comes around again, I don't expect 120 is gonna be the stopping point. It may be 130, 140, 150... I can't imagine any equipment left running outdoors is likely to survive the stress.

So, one year at the most, one month, one week, one day... more likely. (Or, worse comes to worst, there's always the pills on the night table...)

(*TIM stands, walks around.*)

But in the meantime, here's my question to the great beyond. I'm never going to hear the answer to it. Nobody here on Earth is ever going to hear the answer to it. Mars One? Nina? I'm sure you guys must have noticed the lack of communication heading back your way. You get the internet where you are? I know, I know, I know: you've got your hands full, but generations from now, you might want your descendants to be kicking this one around.

Mostly, though... this is for the universe at-large. Klingons? Vulcans, Wookies, Ewoks...? I need this to be non-species-centric.

The question: is this inevitable? Will our technology always outrun our maturity?

Individually, we CAN put our hand on that stove... we have that ABILITY. But most of us reach sufficient cognition before we do any damage with that stove. Likewise: fireworks, alcohol, cars... Sometimes the tiniest touch on the stove, a fender bender with the car, is enough to get us to adjust our behavior.

But as a species? Collectively? As a group we default to the age of ***nine***! We cannot come to the collective conclusion that it's time to stop drinking, to douse our fireworks, and take our foot off the gas.

And so, we race, screaming, off... into the darkness.

Is this the answer that awaits us all? Humans? Klingons? Cockroach/lizard people?

Droids? Maybe droids could figure this out. Hey... They had three laws of robotics. Why didn't we have those programmed into us?

In the billions of worlds that are out there, there must be a tiny fraction that can sustain life. Some develop slowly, they may still be in the amoeba stage... others faster, perhaps much faster than us.

And so, intelligent life... Born like a baby. Into a world of resources, learning to tame the elements. How many times has this already happened since the big bang? Could we possibly be the first? THAT sounds a little arrogant to me. But do they all develop opposable thumbs and learn to walk erect only to blow themselves up, and wipe themselves out?

(*TIM sits during the next line.*)

We've actually had five—well, now, six – extinction events that we know of. Vast numbers of species go out of business, the planet hits the reset button and starts over. Turns out, just because we had brains and shit[8] didn't make us immune or exempt. Or, in the words of the late, great Rick Perry: "Oops!"

So: Is this why we don't have any actual E.T.'s?

---

[8] "Stuff" is always available as an alternative to "shit," as is "crap." Although, I think "shit" has largely worked it's way into the common vernacular by now (thanks to cable television), and there's been a notable reduction of hyperventilating over the use of the word.

Hey! If you're out there! Grow the fuck[9] up, wouldja? Sure, you've evolved over a million years, but watch out for that first internal combustion engine! It's going to bite you in the ass.

Yes, God gave us oil. Or, God gave us trees that got squeezed into oil. Or, God gave us fungus that turned into trees.

But if we're gonna pass the responsibility over to God, then well, well then… God did also give us brains and logical thinking and, ultimately… science. And while it was, to some degree, science (along with the oil and the engine) that got us into this mess, it was also science that showed us the impact that shit was having on air, climate, temperature...

We loved and embraced one aspect of science when it pleased and served us. We reject other aspects that threaten to take our goodies away.

Year in, year out, Earth in, Earth out… Is this a cycle? Will each infant planet come to the same conclusion? *Or is it possible for maturity to outrace technology?*

BLACKOUT.

LIGHTS UP.

How many of you infant sentient species WERE there out there who never made it past that first year as a toddler? How many are out there now, toddling along? How many have been listening to this odd stream of radio waves coming from Earth over the past century? Did you get bored and stop listening? Did you listen long enough to figure out there was some kind of a language there?

Are you listening now?

---

[9] Of course, "hell," "heck," etc., are reasonable alternatives. "Tim's" occasional use of "fuck," here, is intended to remind us that he pretty much has nothing left to lose.

On the off-chance that you're listening now, or, perhaps are recording this as some odd series of bleeps and bloops that you'll play back and translate later… I bleed my words into the abyss...

What DO you think these noises are? Are they God to you? Does God speak to you in bleeps? Probably not if you've been watching American television for the last thirty years.

(*TIM stands, walks around.*)

Okay… let's go with the God thing. Yeah, okay. This is God speaking. Let me think up some commandments…

Okay, here's one: Air Conditioning. Whatever planet you live on, you evolved into a thinking species without air conditioning. Your planet is *by definition, habitable*. Work with it. The impulse to terra-form your planet threatens an immeasurable number of indigenous species upon whose shoulders you stand far more precariously than you might possibly imagine. And I say this as someone who, A,[10] hates spiders, and B, will likely be dead within 24 hours of his air cutting off.

Commandment 2: Stop idling. We drew up laws against idling in our last couple of years. I don't mean laziness, though, of course, there's that. There came a time in which it became impossible to go anywhere outside without driving while running the air conditioner. But once people reached their destination, they couldn't bring themselves to turn the air conditioning off! And, so, they idled… running the most expensive air conditioner ever developed. Belching tons of carbon into the air, just for the sake of cooling down a few cubic feet of space. Towards the end, people were being torn from their cars… but by that time… you get the idea.

---

[10] Acting note: Tim holds up one finger as he says "A", realizes that he should have said "one," but having begun in an alphabetical enumeration, reluctantly holds up two fingers as he continues with "B".

Commandment 3: Do not get too attached to any given technology. Just because you CAN do it, and MIGHT use it, doesn't mean that you OUGHT to. The average round-trip trans-ocean airplane flight has a carbon footprint roughly equivalent to driving the average car through the course of the average year... ***per passenger!*** Eliminating air travel altogether would have been the equivalent of taking, like, a million cars off of the road PER DAY. But, we Pandoraed air travel out of the box, and never even thought about putting it back in! We spent centuries yearning to be as free as birds, and the occasional cavity search for the privilege of sitting in a narrow aluminum tube with liquids of no more than three ounces was just about as close as we were gonna get. But once we had it...!

And lo, there came unto the people the vision of the "Hockey Stick!"

(*TIM sits.*)

Not a commandment... just... um... God, talkin'.

Somewhere around the turn of the millennium, somebody noticed the graph of temperatures was oddly reminiscent of a hockey stick. A long, long, long steady decline, reaching back over maybe *ten thousand years*, followed by a sudden swoop upwards, starting kind of around the industrial revolution, but never widely noticed or articulated until the 21st century. At which point, we all kind of looked at it and said, "wow; yep, that's a warming trend!"

But we thought we still had time.

Because it was a hockey stick! It angled down, and then it angled up. It was still an ANGLE.

People argued about the meaning of the angle; some denied it, but it was still just an angle... We had time to adjust our behavior, make a change, wean our way ever-so-gradually off of the stuff... starting, like first thing tomorrow.

We didn't count on that angle continuing to curve, continuing to accelerate, turning from an angle into... a... a... a plane.

"An exponential growth of anything never looks like very much at first, but then it builds up quite suddenly..."

Things don't happen in isolation.

Things affect other things.[11] And other things change. And those changed things affect the first things, making them worse. And the worse things impact the second things, making them terrible.

And we hit the wall.

In our case the second thing was the methane.

Am I getting too technical with it all? Maybe I should just stop with "things affect other things."

(*TIM stands, walks around.*)

Okay well, quickly: We all knew about carbon. It was clouding the air, creating the greenhouse effect, trapping heat, driving up temperatures. It's a bitch.

And with those rising temperatures, stuff started to melt. We all knew it would swell the oceans and wreck the coastline, and all that happened, slow at first, but then kind of… fast.

But along with the icebergs and the glaciers, there was also the permafrost. Stuff that hadn't melted in, like, ten thousand years was now melting in the course of about 10 years.

All at once.

Releasing methane… Yes: farts, shit, gas, bacteria. Stuff that had been trapped in the permafrost, which was suddenly nowhere near so "perma" as it had been cracked up to be.

---

[11] Tim "locates" any references to "first things" with a gesture toward the left side of the table/desk. The "second things" are always imagined to be on the right side of the desk. Thus when he shifts to "carbon" and "methane," carbon is to the left and methane to the right. (The swelling oceans are "located" in the audience, while the "permafrost" is further off, stage right.)

It turns out methane heats stuff up even more. More ice melts. Less light is reflected away from where ice once was. Which generates **more** heat, kicking off a seemingly never-ending series of forest fires. Which coughs even more carbon into the air, all the while eradicating carbon-reducing/oxygen-producing plant life!

And suddenly, lands that were once capable of bearing crops are now drier than the dust bowl, triggering famine, starvation, sudden spikes of migration, spikes redoubled by the rising sea levels, which, given that 10% of the world population had been living within 30 feet of sea level – and don't get me started on all the nuclear plants parked and eventually abandoned on the shore line – generates yet another flood, this one of refugees!

And, as if that were not enough, the melting permafrost sets free the mothers of all ancient diseases, which, now, like Captain America, are back in the game, hitting us with anthrax, bubonic plague, stuff I'd never heard of and still can't pronounce, financial collapse and the four horsemen of the apocalypse!

Each and every one of these things, sets off each and every part of every other thing, which in turn re-cranks up the original thing. It's a feedback loop!

(*TIM sits.*)

But, for those of us who still can, just blast the air conditioning.

Leave the car running.

Keep flying.

Jack up the shit that was making the problem bad in the first place.

And hold off the refugees as long as you possibly can.

And... shit gets worse, and wars break out.... like overnight.

"And the blood of English shall manure the ground."[12]

---

[12] **Richard II**, Act IV, Scene 1.

Things affect other things. A bedtime story.

Akgh! Shit, shit, shit...! Fuck-fuck-fuck. Shut up, shut up, shut up!

Hey! Sorry! Shake it off!

BLACKOUT.

LIGHTS UP.

Is it possible, is it rational, is it in any way meaningful to fight on behalf of a people you've never met, will never meet? Maybe/probably don't exist?

Iknow-Iknow-Iknow: they're not "people."

They're... let's say: "intelligent life."

Well... anyway, if not that, then what meaning ***can there possibly be***?

Commandment Four:

The cost of buying a thing needs to reflect the expense it inflicts on the planet, at large.

There once was a time when a gallon of gas was less than a dollar. I still remember when it was still less than two dollars.

But that one or two dollars only accounts for the expense of extracting it out of the ground: the pumps and the pipes... the transport, the ads... the lobbyists, lawyers.

Turns out that for each single dollar's extraction, was another, say, two bucks impact-on-the-planet. Just guessing, we were spending a trillion or more every year on the gas.

Two trillion a year should have gone into wetlands, renewables, recyclables trees, vacuuming the crap out of the oxygen... "planet infrastructure."

We learned all of this on a personal scale; when we finally got cigarettes were a poison, we just taxed the shit out of it. Nowhere near enough to quite compensate, but, most of those people were now dead already.

But if every dollar creating the damage was matched by another two bucks for repair? Well, we might well have been a bit more discreet about spending that dollar to start with.

So then, did we tax that one dollar of gas?

No, we ***subsidized*** it.

We dropped down the cost of that dollar's extraction to just about 85 cents. The richest of companies yet known to man now paid out near zero in taxes.

We collectively said, "Hey, we need all this shit to survive and succeed, and these bastions of commerce… are risking their assets for magic elixirs that make our things go! They must be… underwritten! Let us give them great grants and rewards… the shiniest metals for making the wheels of our industry turn, as they churn rich black smoke on up into the air.

Which brings up Number Five.

Those who make up your laws must not profit therein. Because each single time, they will bow to your magic elixir of profit far more than that vague and uncertain voodoo that your eggheads call science, forcing the three trillion cost of their gas on down to a most unsustainable one.

Side note.

Still god, here, so listen.

Money is not a thing.

It's a concept.

Which we bring in to stand for those things we could have. If only we just had the money.

And those things themselves… are not things.

(*TIM stands, walks around.*)

They are representations of joy we have lost, love we have lost. The creative spark that has gone out on us. If I've enough things, if I can fly like a bird, or race in my car against time till those feelings return. Love, joy, sparks, tingles… those lost moments from back in the day when I used to deserve.

(*Pause… leans in to microphone…*)

Still waiting on that "ding" any time anyone might well want to weigh in.

Really? Sweden? New Zealand? There's somebody there in New Zealand, right?

Okay, well, then, it's me and Proxima Centauri… or Termina Centauri. Or some place in between. My voice goes out and you hear it in, what, thirty years? Three thousand or so? And then you'll talk back? And sixty, six thousand years from this tick you'll talk to a very hot planet in your unique accent in your own special… diction.

Of course, I won't be here. Nobody will. And you'll have learned English for no good reason. Unless, maybe you manage to download some Shakespeare.

But the planet itself won't be dead.

Sure, the roads will all crumble, the buildings collapse, and maybe the last living things to survive will be cockroaches, and some fungi.

You might find yourself talking to some really fun-gi!

Sorry.

It'll all go to shit for a time, and a thousand years more… or maybe a million, the earth has a cleanse. It rains and it buries the carbon below once again. And the skyscrapers form some new form of bedrock, and the fun-guys form life or the lizards form brains, become Klingons.

And THEN! You'll have someone to talk to from here.

Except they'll speak Klingon, and it won't that much matter 'cause they'll all have sprung from primordial ooze and won't retain even the tiniest fraction of the INSTITUTIONAL MEMORY I have with me now! YOU could, if you wanted, catch them up on things…

(*TIM sits.*)

So... this is one-way. As much you might find you want to respond to someone quite so CHARISMATIC as me, by the time you reply, I just won't be all that much into you then, so maybe just listen: I'm no kind of genius; just the last one to witness to things not quite costing as much as they probably ought: cross-reference to rule number four.

So… sex.

Sex was kind of important to us. Probably is to you, too. It tingles. Feels good. And you want to repeat what feels good… so you relive the success of your sex in successive conceptions. If it don't feel so good, then you're not so inspired to re-seed the species and your special branch of the prolific process simply won't stretch itself out so far.

But for us, it was good. Really good. I remember it.

I still engage in it from time to time. Not quite in a way you could quite call productive.[13]

But, boy, were we productive!

(*TIM stands, walks around.*)

And our sudden explosion of *reproductive matter* outpaced, or *edged out* all the stuff gone before us.

---

[13] This somewhat oblique reference can be dropped if it's too scandalous for your community standards.

We toddled along with maybe a million a really long time. Till that whole *farming thing*, you know, kind of took off. We had a slight hitch around 1300 when the bubonic plague... But we figured out hygiene, and got back to work. We hit our first billion around 1800. Number two? 1920. And then 1960, and 75, 1990, 2000, 2010, 2020. In just 60 years, we tacked on FIVE BILLION to double and triple the cumulative efforts of a hundred fifty thousand long years as a species!

The sex was, yeah, good!

But without precedent! We were only just *guessing* that we could sustain at this pace!

We were a great throng of sex-starved adolescents, making all of it up as we toddled along! Extra billion? Why not? Never mind at the same time we're using, well, food! We made up this sudden new craving for gas. For electric. For power. We needed it. Craved it. It got us to shelter, it got us more comfort, it got us more sex!

Some countries *encouraged* their folks reproduce... It provided protection against other states, other kinds, that great horde of those swarthy barbarians.

And then, we again, put our words in God's mouth: "Be fruitful and multiply!"

And there for a little brief time that paid off.

Until, well it didn't.

(*TIM sits.*)

So, rule number **six**: Don't get over your skis. Grow only to where you can sustain the thread. Expanding to unheard-of numbers the same time demand has run multiple laps blowing past all the output of all time gone by? Really a risky maneuver.

Sure, easy for me to say now! Boy, when I was your age, I was some raconteur!

Which is great. Share affection and love. Just don't multiply as if it were a race. 'Cause, to coin a phrase: that's a race to the bottom! (More ways than one.)

(Pauses to see if anyone has gotten the joke. Realizing that he will never actually know, he moves on…)

When you hit the point that the size of your species doubles and triples in less than one lifetime? Take your foot off the gas … find… alternative ways to stimulate such an… addictive sensation… I don't know why I'm embarrassed to talk dirty to some other species.

So, speaking of races:

At each stage of the game, you find that you're faced with illusion of some competition. It's us against those not blessed by God; or us against the barbarians; it's us against the spotted owl; it's us against the Zika virus.

Okay, maybe that one. But on the whole, not.

We came to the random conclusion we were caught up in some competition! If I climb the ladder, I have the advantage, and fill up my pockets with money (*that now is worth nothing*), and pull up the ladder behind me.

There once was a time things were random… a roll of the dice, where each roll might come up one-through-six.

But we started to roll most all sixes. More often than not, each year: hotter than that gone before. The hottest year ever: how often do we get even *one* of those? All things being equal: well, once. Sometimes we would still roll a three or a four, so some would say: see! Random! Not man! It was God! (Of course, that assumes it was God rolling lower for us and not simply smiting our sins of excess with his sixes.)

(*TIM stands during the next line, walks around.*)

And we'd roll one more six, and another, 'cept now all those sixes were closer to *twelves*, and we left any semblance of random behind in an unspoken pact to never acknowledge the screamingly impossible improbability.

Number seven: Acknowledge. Screamingly impossible. Improbabilities.

We grew brains over eons, forged a language or two, developed… statistical analysis, if only so that, you know, the insurance companies could figure out how much to charge us.

There was that time people seemed to forget the principal point of insurance...

They famously said: "Hey, our healthiest people are stuck paying out for the sick!"

That should have been a clue. That all we had left was the ongoing struggle for privilege.

We were all of us grabbing for stuff off the beverage cart in the few final moments before the airplane would crash to the ground.

Acquiring more stuff in the desperate race to fill that black hole that was all we now had left inside.

Everybody kicks in. Each one loses a little. And no one gets thrown off the ship. We extend that principle to owls and bees and coral reefs. **Each one arrives**. We'll make that number eight.

BLACKOUT.

LIGHTS UP.

Okay, here's the thing:

(*TIM sits.*)

I'm kidding myself. I talk to a "you" that I'll never know, broadcast to a planet that lives in my brain. And even if there might yet be some "you" in some state of awareness in some somehow survivable planet out there…

Even if you're out there, the odds I catch you in the brief micro-second of geo/astro/physical time in which you're equipped to get radio waves, but haven't as yet blown yourselves off the map, are maybe a billion to one.

And yet, microscopic as those odds might be... they are not yet zero.

And as far away as you are...

Maybe separation is just an illusion.

Maybe difference is an illusion.

...Communication is an illusion.

Maybe me, sitting here, working through all this shit on some empty planet with no one to hear, at least stirs a shift here... in me.

And maybe my shift in some way, somehow, somewhere is felt... say, Tralfamadore, a planet so far and so very much different from me.

And perhaps that far corner, that ugly unrecognizable race of Tralfamadorians, somehow, yet *is* me. Is connected. By some yet not knowable thread.

A thread as unknowable to me here now as radio waves were two hundred years past.

Or, not.

Likely not.

Number **nine**.

Corporations are made up of people, my friend, but cannot be people. A robot may well be no part human being.

But robots can't consciously "injure a human or, through some inaction allow that a human might so come to harm."

Corporations must act to maximize profit, or otherwise risk getting sued by investors.

It was under this dictate corporations had hid what they were well aware would heat up the planet and leave it a wasteland.

So which of these two would you call "terminator?" Which one of these is more like people, "my friend?"

Which of these has the freedom to obey the commandment to "Do unto others as you would have them likewise do unto you."

Okay, number ten.

We ignore it all until we can't.

And then it's too late.

Deep down we all knew where it was we were headed and what we most needed to do to correct it.

Look, we had freedom. And freedom, yeah, freedom is awesome.

Let's just say that we hadn't quite yet hit the impasse that ended the advantage of comforts we'd come to enjoy.

Unilateral surrender of coveted comforts would mean sharp defeat in the harsh competition of conspicuous consumption we were all convinced we were caught in.

So we shrug and enjoy what's yet left, while sighing, "Well, it's too late now."

The inertia has gathered a force of such strength, no action I take now could save anything. It's now just a *fait accompli*.

And instead of the struggle, we indulge that much more, if only to get past this issue that's hanging uncomfortably, awkwardly over our heads. Like the diet that only now serves to remind you of just how much you like French fries!

We're effectively telling the next generation they should just go eff themselves.

While I might want to give up and jump off that cliff, I've no ethical right to pull all those others along in my wake.

If the best I might offer is but one more day to the next generation, then I owe them that day, or that hour, that minute.

The last generation, on the worst of their days, did at least... as much... as that... for me.

(*Pause.*)

Which is easy for me, here, to say.

I score kind of poorly on "plays well with others."

Look, I had my job; it demanded some travel. I got good results and I made people happy. I was making a difference. I mostly meant well... I tried to recycle. Well, when it was convenient.

I planned out this move here up north. I followed the patterns of temperature, methane and made my best guess. I bought up some land and hollowed the hill, insulated it, filled the largest of pantries with so many cans that I look like I'm living inside Andy Warhol's worst nightmare. I once kind of liked it. But now it all tastes like water with wet chunks of cardboard.

It's not infinite. At best, the supplies could last me some one or two years.

I bolstered the door with lead lining and bolts and I kept on with driving my route...

Until that day arrived, half the country on fire, and there was just no going back past the border. Or at least no excuse to continue.

So I pushed on back north and locked in.

And here, on my screen, saw the myriad fires as they swept cross the plains... For a while they would fight with the fires, and then they just ran.

And from inside my hill I saw all this unfold...

And I sealed up my door, and I shut myself in, and hoped no one would notice the door in the side of a hill now encircled by odd solar panels that gave shade to a lone air conditioning unit, which continued to run in the service of nothing.

It was almost as if some dead miser had furnished his sepulcher with central air.

Which, if not true yet, it will quite soon be, almost any moment from now.

DING, WHY DON'T YOU? WHY DON'T YOU DING, ALREADY???!

Sorry. So.

These things drew attention. As the crowds fled the heat and the fires, and the sense that their brains were now boiling inside of their heads, they worked north, and more north. A handful or so would trip over my door.

They weren't stupid: a door, solar panels, the hum of a fan. They knew I was there.

And some would walk past; a few would hold up, and put it together.

> (*Knocking on the table with each successive description of the ongoing knocking, growing louder, as they knock with knuckles, fists and eventually, slamming with open palms.*)

And knock on the door.

Politely at first.

And then a bit more firmly. Apologetic. Insistent. "Helloooo?" "Is there anyone hooome?"

They lingered a little and went on their way. More came, and heat grew, and the knocks became pounds and the tone of the voice would become much more strained, and "Hellos?" turned to "Hey!" and "***We're dying out here!***"

And I watched, as I sat, and I froze in my place. My most temperate place. Where I would survive as but one man alone.

Because stores for two years for one man will only last one year for two, or six months for four, or three months for eight. And once letting in one, I'd no way to restrain just how many more might yet squeeze on in through.

So… all that stuff I just said…

Sounds good in the abstract. Until it's just you. And the others. And suddenly… yes, it is competition… between you, and the others. Who get thrown off the ship. 'Cause we *don't* all quite get there together!

So… all that stuff I just said…

Was just stuff I just said.

So. Take those commandments, for just what they're worth.

'Cause, they don't come from God.

Just a guy.

Who failed at each step to step up to each one.

But maybe you get ahead of the curve… of the hockey stick curve that turns into a wall. And adjust your behavior. Before all you see is how it's turned now: each man for himself.

You can watch for the signs.

Insurance. Watch for insurance. If you can't work out that one, then it just will not work.

Or perhaps plant a tree. Or a trillion some trees.

Just do me one favor.

Record this and send it ahead. To the next. And the next. To the Klingons, the Vulcans, the Tralfamadorians. Pass it on. Maybe… just maybe, we'll catch someone in time.

I'm done. I'm going to bed. I have doubts on if I'll be getting back up.

(*TIM stands, leans into the microphone.*)

This is Tim, signing off: August 17, 2028.

(*Note adjust date to be exactly 10 years after the date of performance.*)

(*TIM exits, hesitates halfway to door, glancing back at the computer, and continues to exit.*)

(*The computer "dings".*)

(*It "dings" more.*)

(*The digs segue into curtain call music.*)

BLACKOUT

Post-show Discussion/Commentary/Exegesis

"Sending these signals out into the universe" *(page 3)*
This has been a trope of sci-fi for many years. Yes, these signals do reach out relatively unimpeded into the universe. Perhaps they have been received. Perhaps not. Perhaps those of advanced technological capability have responded. Perhaps not. Perhaps they have responded with an actual return visit. That, of course, would demand an *extremely* advanced technology, one which we, ourselves, have not achieved, and one which, as this play suggests, may be ultimately impossible, in light of the position we now find ourselves in.

"Bang. Zoom. To the moon, Alice!" *(p. 3)*
Given that the TV show, "The Honeymooners" is a product of the 1950s, I am reminded that the youthful public-at-large may not know who they are. Of course it is easy to Google this material, but the relevant point is that Ralph Cramden would occasionally threaten his wife with the possibility that he might actually hit her, supposedly so strongly that it would send her into outer space, or, "to the moon." (Yes, it is a product of America's patriarchal history, but, for the most part, we were never intended to side with Ralph over his wife, Alice.)

"Northern Canada north." *(p. 4)*
For what it's worth, I have no idea if this (building a bunker in Northern Canada) is a viable strategy for surviving climate disaster. The only thing that really matters is that Tim thought it might be, and got lucky somehow. If you can call this "lucky."

"Mars Colony One; are you out there?" *(p. 5)*
As Tim chats idly into the microphone (before hitting the rhythm of the "deep dives" into the several themes he expounds upon at length), he tends to jump around to whatever topic strikes him next. In this instance, "flat Earthers" reminds him of the self-evidently ***round*** view of Earth from outer space, and those two other potential audiences now viewing earth from those two greater distances.

"Never quite relocate Cape Canaveral in time" *(p. 5)*
Cape Canaveral, of course, on the Eastern Florida coast, would have been rendered unusable by the rising seas and ravaging storms. Similarly, many of our nuclear power facilities, almost always built on

the shoreline, would find themselves threatened by the rising seas. It is worth revisiting the stories of the damage caused by the tsunami that struck Japan in 2011. The reactors were successfully shut down, but the power was cut, disabling the emergency generators and releasing radioactive materials. This was, of course, a one-time, localized disaster. If and when the seas rise, that will be a world-wide event which will re-draw shorelines permanently (or for, say, thousands of years).

"Too fast for my voice to catch up." *(p. 5)*
Given that "Tim" is as ignorant as I am in these matters, I have not corrected the mistake that I have learned since first writing this scene, as a physics teacher subsequently informed me that radio waves travel, not at the speed of sound, but at the speed of light. As such, these signals will eventually catch up to ships traveling at less than the speed of light. But, even if such signals have already reached them, neither Tim, nor we, have any sense of whether those folks, preoccupied as they are, might be listening.

"D.C. ... lit up like a tinderbox" *(p. 6)*
There are several references similar to "D.C. lit up like a tinderbox" scattered through this play. What was clearly a horrifying calamity at the time has been reduced to the shrug of an afterthought. It's intended to introduce a tension between an audience's fears of the coming cataclysm and the future survivors' need to cope with what's next.

"Nurturing genetic code" *(p. 7)*
I believe that the argument of evolution is inextricably tied to the understanding of climate change. If we cannot bring ourselves to an understanding and acceptance of the notion that life, the environment and humanity itself was somehow fundamentally different in centuries or millennia gone by (or perhaps even to accept that there was indeed "millennia gone by"), then it will be particularly difficult to envision the human race on a continuum that starts with "not existing" - shifts to "existing" - and potentially returns to "not existing" again.

Those who are freaked out about any evolutionary connection with "monkeys" quite possibly see the human race as divinely endowed to whimsically wreak any destruction on the planet they might wish, without any threat of either karmic retribution or the fallout from actual human impact on a fragile environment.

As such, I repeatedly, unapologetically, revisit the known scientific facts of evolution to firmly remind the evolution deniers that "all the cool kids" understand without question that we live on a fragile planet that exists in continuous flux.

To be clear, I take no position on the existence of God. I just don't happen to believe that God endorses purposeful ignorance or the assumption that the world will continue to endure the impact of craven exploitation and arrogance without consequence.

"How arrogant of you, you puny humans..." *(p. 8)*
The parallel thesis to the resistance of evolution is the climate deniers' argument that humans, themselves, are incapable of impact on the grand scale of planet-level disturbance. We are, of course, little people: tiny dwarfs in the grand scale of a very large planet. How could we ever possibly effect a shift in the fragile balance that has allowed us to evolve over the past millennia?

Of course, that seems like a viable argument until you consider that it is not so much a human series of impacts so much as a series of human choices to relocate the carbon remnants of many thousands of years from their underground refuges into the atmosphere. Not the impact of one puny human, but of some eight billion humans that find themselves, as a collective mass, ever more desperately dependent on those addictive carbons.

These are, of course, actual arguments that come up in the face of science that we don't like: A) "It would be arrogant to even suggest that I might have such power as to do this kind of damage," and B) "I am not meant to understand." This is a natural but inevitably corrupt human impulse that has its roots in the same attitude that produces the "prosperity gospel," which suggests that "If I am rich, there must be some inherent virtue in me which inspired God to make me rich." The inverse-but-closely-related impulse is captured in the famous Upton Sinclair quote (also quoted by Al Gore in "An Inconvenient Truth") "It is difficult to get a man to understand something when his salary depends upon his not understanding it."

"500... no 600 parts-per-million." *(p. 9)*
As of this writing (August, 2018), the level of carbon in the air is roughly 412.5 parts per million. For years, scientists had warned that the 400 ppm threshold, higher than any level in at least one million

years, would be indicative of severe climate disaster. We passed that milestone in May of 2013, and seem to be accelerating. Tim's inability to remember the precise current number suggests the continued acceleration of this figure, and our casual inattention to its unprecedented growth.

"It may be 130, 140, 150..." *(p. 9)*
Clearly, Tim is not a scientist, here, and has no idea about exact temperatures or precise interactions of the factors driving these astonishing temperatures. He's simply someone who recognized a trend and took steps toward self-preservation. Will next year's temperature jump add an incredible 30 degrees to an already unthinkable heat wave? I don't know any better than he does.

And yet, part of the point is that none of us know. Even the most informed and brilliant scientists can only estimate what might happen when hitherto unprecedented levels of carbon, methane and who-knows-what-else interact.

But assuming ***no*** interaction or change in the environment, or some unprecedented intervention of divine benevolence would be blindingly irresponsible.

"Will our technology always outrun our maturity?" *(p. 9)*
This is another theme to which I will repeatedly return: The maturity/life cycle of the individual vs. the maturity/life cycle of the collective.

Early on, within the course of a dozen years or so, we realize, individually, that certain behaviors, thought perhaps pleasurable in the impulse of the moment, will ultimately lead to bad ends.

But when reckless behavior leads to a collective "bad end" we are often trapped in a kind of a "prisoners dilemma:" two prisoners, cross-examined individually might go free if both refuse to confess. But the lack of faith in the other's choices leads one (or both) to rat out the other in hopes of a better deal. Likewise, our ongoing lack of faith in those other individuals that compose "society" leads us to grab for our own "better deal" (e.g., limitless energy consumption) before it gets swept from the table.

Is this the inevitable result of having an individuated consciousness? Will each planet on which intelligent life develops ultimately turn to self-absorbed, destructive behavior? Is there any hope to altering the seemingly inescapable nature of consciousness and self-absorption?

"Three laws of robotics" *(Page 10)*
The three laws of Robotics as created by Dr. Isaac Asimov for his series of books about robots (most notably, "I, Robot") include:

1) A robot may not injure a human being or, though inaction, allow a human being to come to harm.
2) A robot must obey orders given it by human beings, except where such orders would conflict with the First Law.
3) A robot must protect its own existence as long as such protection does not conflict with the first or second law.

Obviously having such laws "programmed into us" might have saved us from many of the machinations that have threatened our existence. But that whole "obey orders" clause would almost certainly have been a deal-killer.

"Extinction Events" *(p. 10)*
Since history is so vast and evolution seemingly so slow (we humans have gone through significant changes in size and diet, over just the last fifty years, and those happen, largely, without our noticing, even within our own lifetimes), it's good to be reminded of the precarious perch upon which we stand.

Information drawn from "WorldAtlas.com":

1) 439 Million years ago: 86% of Earth's life wiped out, probably due to falling sea levels and extreme glacial coverage (Known as the Ordovican-Silurian Extinction)
2) 364 Million years ago: 75% of species lost as plant life depleted the seas of oxygen and, therefore, animal life. (Late Devonian Extinction)
3) 251 Million years ago: 96% of species lost due to an enormous volcanic eruption which filled the air with carbon dioxide (and, eventually, methane). (Permian-Triassic Extinction)
4) 200 Million years ago: An asteroid impact tipped the scale from mammal dominance to dinosaur dominance (enabling

dinosaurs to evolve relatively unimpeded for 135 million years). (Triassic-Jurassic Extinction)

5) 65 Million years ago: 76% of life destroyed by a combination of asteroid and volcanic eruption, wiping out dinosaurs and leaving mammals. (Cretaceous-Paleogene extinction)

6) 120 years ago-Present Day: "Nearly half of mammal species surveyed lost more than 80% of their distribution," likely due to human overpopulation and overconsumption.[14] (Holocene Extinction)

Just as individual beings live, die and are replaced, likewise entire species grow to fulfillment and die out. We can imagine (actual scientists have likely measured) just how many millennia it took for the dinosaurs to grow to the enormity they eventually achieved. However tiny their brains, I would certainly expect that they, too, assumed that their species was a divinely generated given circumstance that would continue through all time (i.e., I don't think they saw extinction coming). In the meantime, our efforts to date the Earth's history on a Biblical schedule (some 6,000 years) forces us into a wildly optimistic view of planetary history, narrowing it to that very tiny band of time in which we humans, violent as we may be, have been on a particularly good "winning streak."

"Trees that got squeezed into oil... Fungus which turned into trees..." *(p. 12)*

This is, obviously, a simplistic look at the evolutionary/botanic/petro-chemical process, but Tim is a somewhat simple guy when it comes to the nuances of science. (Assumedly, most of our audience are not ready for much detail either.) However, as Tim will soon remind us, plants absorb carbon. Those plants find themselves buried over the centuries, trapped under rock, silt and sediment, where geothermal heating "squeezes" that plant life into the brew we know as "oil." Of course, over the last century or so, we have been extracting that oil from the ground, recirculating it into the air in the form of carbon exhaust far faster than the eons leading to its initial burial. As a result the ratio of

---

[14] This is a much-shortened/somewhat-paraphrased listing of the materials presented on the Worldatlas.com article: "Timeline Of Mass Extinction Events On Earth." The specific quote regarding mammal species in Event #6 is drawn from an article posted on theguardian.com: "Earth's sixth mass extinction event under way, scientists warn", July 10, 2017.

carbon to oxygen is far greater than it has been (as far as we can tell) for a million years or more.

BLACKOUT *(p. 12)*
The blackouts are intended to provide the tiniest pause (just a couple of seconds) to give some sense that time has passed. In this instance, Tim has completed one of his trademark riffs, finishing off one major theme. The brief pause allows us to hit a "reset" button, of sorts, if only to keep Tim from seeming to be some impossible wizard/genius who composes endless, elaborate, spiraling essays off of the top of his head.

For all we know, several hours or several days may have passed. (Given that Tim will not have enough time to change costume, we will probably assume several hours.)

"The God Thing" *(p. 13)*
Writer's note: Up until this point much of this material has been a somewhat scattershot reflection of the random ideas that flutter through Tim's brain. With "the God thing…" Tim has finally hit upon the theme that will carry him through the remainder of this play (which is true of Tim-the-Writer as well as Tim-the-Character).

Commandment 1: "Air Conditioning" *(p. 13)*
Air conditioning may be one of the lesser contributors to global warming (the carbon expelled in heating homes during cold weather is generally worse), but the fears and challenges of going without air conditioning are so severe that using air conditioning (and, more broadly, "terra-forming") as a starting point may help soften up our audience to notions of self-sacrifice. It's also a key lead-in to our second commandment which is much more directly connected to the release of carbon into the atmosphere.

Commandment 2: "Idling" *(p. 13)*
Given that Tim is now up on his feet, I (in my performance) generally return to the chair at this moment to scope out the "few cubic feet of space" that a seated body actually occupies, shaping the air occupied by that imaginary body with my hands. This "commandment" adds to the need for sacrifice introduced above with the somewhat more ominous threat of violence that is likely to surface as the mid or post-apocalyptic society approaches the brink.

Commandment 3: "Any given technology" *(p. 13)*
Tim is engaging in a significant bit of dramatic rounding/exaggerating. A search of statistics on this will find this information framed in multiple dizzying ways, and clouded with internal arguments about the way such statistics need to be framed. The actual comparison may find the round-trip trans-ocean flight having a carbon footprint 50% (or less) of the average-car-per-year footprint (4.6 metric tons). Obviously the departure/arrival locations of your flight will greatly vary the impact. To calculate your own planned travel, go to carbonfootprint.com to find much more detailed figures. My goal in expressing these figures with such round numbers is largely to wake ourselves up to the need to consider and study the impact of *any* technological advances... especially flying.

Side note: My self-imposed rule it generally to round my numbers up or down to the nearest factor of ten, as Tim uses 10,000, 100,000, a million or "a billion" to make his points. Whenever I find that he is off by more than that, I adjust the number upwards or downwards. Tim is not a scientist, and this is not an adjudicated scientific paper. While there is truth behind these numbers, Tim is expressing himself in the "gesture" of such citations. It matters less that we know that the ratio of annual auto carbon to one-time airplane carbon is a particular fraction, than that they are closely relatable in the first place!

"A million cars" *(p. 13)*
This is, of course, another broad estimate, based on the roughly four billion flights taken each year (10 million-plus people flying each day). Of course, some are much shorter trips than others. Under current trends, however, that figure is expected to ***double*** over the next twenty years. And we have not yet found (probably will never find) a way to build commercial airplanes that fly on renewable sources. This estimate works from the previously cited 4.6 metric tons figure... In other words, one full year of a car not driving on the road, accumulated through the course of the year, or some 300 million cars off of the road in a single year (coincidentally, roughly equivalent to the population of the United States, and perhaps three times the number of cars currently in the U.S.). For reference, there are an estimated 1.015 billion cars currently (2018) in use, worldwide.

One friend, by the way, challenged me on this discussion: "But it's impossible to just stop flying." And I was instantly reminded of the fact that we actually *did* stop flying in the three days following the 9/11 terror attack. It was incredibly inconvenient, but we survived. Which is more than we can say about an extinction event. (Note: there is ongoing discussion about whether the "contrails" that follow airplanes actually contribute to, or take away from, global warming. Some suggest that they reflect sunlight away from the earth during the day, and trap heat at night. I include this discussion largely to suggest that we are capable of what may be a significant amount of sacrifice when the need presses us. Ultimately, solving this will demand a nuanced strategy developed by scientists, not dramatists.)

"Oddly reminiscent of a hockey stick." *(p. 13)*
While "Tim" doesn't know who this is, it was Michael E. Mann, Raymond S. Bradley and Malcom K. Hughes who developed the statistical techniques to measure average temperatures (eventually) reaching back over 10,000 years, which created the now-famous "hockey stick graph," and climatologist Jerry Mahlman who coined the term "hockey stick" to describe it's shape.

"An exponential growth of anything..." *(p. 13)*
The end of this quote is, "...and suddenly you're kind of fleeing for your life." (Peter Wadham, as interviewed on the Thom Hartman Show, September 25, 2017.)

"Things Affect Other Things" ("A Bedtime Story") *(p. 14)*
This is the heart of the argument upon which this play is based. We mostly understand the impact of carbon by now, and how its growing presence in the atmosphere creates the greenhouse effect and drives up temperature. (This has factored into past "extinction events" that we know of.)

However, as discussed here, there is an unknowable secondary impact when that melting ice releases methane off into the atmosphere. Methane was at the heart of a couple of other past extinction events as well. (See pages 35-36.)

This give and take of two impactful factors is the centerpiece of research and forecasting developed by Guy McPherson, "the worlds leading authority on Near-Term Extinction," and author of the blog/website/video series, "Nature Bats Last."

Guy's predictions in this area suggest an even faster race into climate degradation, and my only excuse for avoiding the sudden calamity that

Guy is now predicting is my own desperate (perhaps naïve) need for hope in the belief that some immediate corrective action might actually stem this disaster.

We have only begun coming to terms (and awareness of the notion) that melting ice leads to rising ocean levels, increased hurricane activity and greater flooding (especially in low-lying "terra-formed" cities such as Miami and Houston). We are still (as I write this in 2018) in a kind of state of denial as we continue to hope that next year's hurricane season will be less devastating than the previous year. Of course, some let-up of this onslaught is still possible, but it is just as possible that we will go from last year's array of five Category-Five storms to six or seven. Or, perhaps, that meteorologists will suddenly need to define a storm-level of Category Six.

One week prior to writing these thoughts, a hurricane in the Atlantic Ocean disappeared off of the north end of the hurricane tracking grid (which had been set in such a way that did not anticipate such extreme high winds reaching as far north as Ireland). The casual off-handedness of Tim's "slow at first, and then… kind of fast" is intended to reflect the sudden surety in which what has been a controversial argument becomes the terrifying new status quo.

Rather than desperately clinging to the hope and the argument that this may all still go away, my intent here is to jump past the pretense of argument to a moment in time in which climate change is as obvious and undeniable as "the nose on your face."

"The Mothers of All Ancient Diseases…" *(Page 14)*
Following years of struggle, a first anthrax vaccine for cows was developed in 1881 by Louis Pasteur, eventually followed by a vaccine for a human anthrax in 1954, largely bringing an end to the devastation the disease had wreaked on the public (although it has sometimes since then been used as a tool of bioterrorism).

In August of 2016, there was an outbreak of anthrax, killing one child and hospitalizing dozens in Siberia. The source of the disease was traced back to a reindeer, which, 75-years before, had died of anthrax poisoning, leaving the carcass frozen under a thin layer of permafrost. The melting permafrost released re-animated spores of anthrax into the air. In some areas, the permafrost is more than 1,000 feet deep (the height of the Empire State Building), and more deposits of Spanish flu, smallpox and the bubonic plague are likely present. (NPR.org, "Anthrax Outbreak in Russia Thought To Be The Result Of Thawing Permafrost," August 3, 2016)

Of course disease outbreak is just one of the unexpected, largely un-anticipatable, consequences of melting ice and rising seas.

"Commandment Four: The Cost of Buying a Thing..." *(p. 16)*
The incentive structure for keeping the cost of gasoline artificially low has forced us into an upside-down "bizzaro-world" carbon dependency, even in an era of scientific wizardry in which entire cities and even countries have committed to (and sometimes accomplished) 100% renewable fuel sourcing.

At the heart of the issue is the grip of established corporate power in a political landscape that allows what amounts to outright bribery, as corporations have proven willing to issue steady streams of cash financing to political action committees tied to parties and politicians.

At a time in which certain businesses need to be winding down and closing up shop (if the planet is to have any hope of survival) our political system pours ever more support into fossil fuel industries, supercharging these businesses with grants, subsidies and tax breaks while scaling back hard-won mileage and emissions goals... even as I type this.

"Two Trillion a Year..." *(p. 16)*
Again, these numbers are more the product of a convenient, graspable equation than an actual measure of specific spending needs. Of course, the longer we go without mitigating the devastating effects of carbon release, the greater the expense of restoring the planet to a manageable shape (a cost that will continue to rise until such time as environmental management becomes entirely impossible).

When I first wrote this scene, I had, somewhere in the back of my mind, a recollection of oil subsidies that I assumed were a quaint misstep of the past. I thought I was making fun of a past mistake of upside-down priorities.

As I researched, I was shocked to read that, world-wide, ***here in 2018***, there was perhaps as much as one trillion spent, not on the cost of the fuel itself, but for government subsidies to reduce the overall cost of that extraction, pointedly "not including other costs of fossil fuels related to climate change, environmental impacts, military conflicts and spending, and health impacts." (Priceofoil.org/fossil-fuel-subsidies) The current administration is working even *more* actively to drive the tax burden on oil companies down to zero.

Of course, these numbers all get at the issue in differing ways, measuring different issues, but certainly the ballpark of "a trillion dollars" is not an overly-generous estimate.
Of late, some have begun to promote potential technologies which might extract or "vacuum" carbons out of the air, potentially formulating it into another form of gasoline... This, unfortunately, would likely only *sustain*, but not reduce, current carbon levels (assuming it is ever launched on a massive world-wide scale).

"We finally got cigarettes were a poison" *(p. 17)*
There was a memorable moment in 1994, in which seven CEOs of the major tobacco corporations unanimously testified before congress, under oath, that cigarettes (and nicotine) were ***not*** addictive. The public reaction was furious (just about all of us knew better by now), and in subsequent years, tobacco industry memos were uncovered demonstrating that "Big Tobacco" had known of the addictive properties of their product for many years, and had even manipulated the ingredients of their product for many years to *maximize* their addictive properties.

Over the following six years, the courts reached massive rulings against the industry with hundreds of millions in compensation for victims and further billions demanded to fund anti-smoking ad campaigns to alert the public to the true impact of smoking.

The corporations warned that such stringent penalties would bankrupt them, although, in the decades since, they have shifted their sales strategies to less litigious third-world markets where they can distribute their product with greater impunity.

Similar documentation regarding "Big Oil's" awareness of the impact of fossil fuels on climate change has now begun to emerge.

One more similarity between the industries: No individual case of lung cancer can be definitively attributed to smoking (given that people who don't smoke *also* get lung cancer), just as no individual hurricane or outrageously hot week of record-breaking temperature can be definitively attributed to increased carbon in the air. It's a situation that forces scientists (and weather-broadcasters) into an extremely passive voice when they describe the extremity of conditions. (See "Commandment Seven" discussion, pgs. 47.)

And sometimes - actually quite often - it so happens that the advertisers who sponsor the news just happen to be petrochemical corporations.

"The richest of companies..." *(p. 17)*
Among the top ten corporations of the Fortune 500 (2018), five are petroleum/ utility companies and two are auto-makers.

Commandment Five: "Must not profit therein..."
The 2010 "Citizens United" Supreme Court decision essentially unleashed a torrent of unrestricted corporate funding of political campaigns, making politicians almost entirely beholden to their corporate sponsors. This decision, when read in light of the assumption that "corporations are people" (pgs. 48-50) has proven to be a formula for inevitable corruption.

"Proxima Centauri" (*p. 18*)
This is a star name that I thought I was making up as I wrote this scene. As it turns out it is the nearest star to the Earth, often overlooked by its more famous neighbor, "Alpha Centauri." Termina Centauri, it turns out *is* a name I made up. (In Tim's mind, at least, "Termina Centauri" is at the far end of the galaxy.)

"The roads will all crumble..." *(p. 18)*
I highly recommend the book, "The World Without Us," (Alan Weisman, St. Martin's Press, New York, 2008), which chases down the thought experiment of "What would happen if humans suddenly stopped inhabiting the earth?" (It turns out things fall apart very quickly, and even the proud metropolis of Manhattan will be reduced (enhanced?) to wilderness in shockingly short order.

"If you want to destroy a barn,' a farmer once told me, "cut an eighteen-inch square hold in the roof. Then stand back.'" (Architect Chris Riddle, as quoted in "The World Without Us," page 15)

Weisman goes on the explain that the barn roof in question will likely be "gone inside of 10 years. Your house's lasts maybe 50 years; 100 tops."

"Without us" things will climb in from above or crawl in from below. The most towering skyscraper will falter and fall without an infrastructure to keep it in place, as once functional cities are flooded, and water, wind, soil, fauna and animal find their way to fill in every flaw that already exists or that develops through the inevitable corrosion of rust, or the absence of functioning systems keeping nature at bay.

Or, as Guy McPherson says, "Nature Bats Last."

"...the success of your sex in successive conceptions..." *(p. 19)*
Actor's note: Tim is not actually this brilliant. As he starts this paragraph, he has no idea just how much the meter of the speech will take hold of him, or precisely how he will find himself adding alliteration to his odd word choices. In other words: he is just as surprised to hear just how exquisitely these words emerge from his mouth as we are. (Ironic that this comes out of him moments after he declares himself "no kind of genius.")

"We toddled along..." *(p. 20)*
There are a few great YouTube videos on overpopulation available: "Human Population Through Time" depicts a series of dots added to the map of the world, essentially from 1 AD through the present. At first we see a smattering of dots around the Mediterranean, India and China, with just the tiniest spots in Africa and the Americas. There is a rare reversal between 1300 and 1400 from the "black death," but as the map crosses over the one billion mark (around 1800), the effect is suddenly like watching a fireworks display. Toward the end, yellow dots cover large masses of the earth.

"In just 60 years..." *(p. 20)*
A quick note on the math: if the population in 1960 was three billion, and the population in 2020 is eight billion, then, yes, the population will have more than doubled in 60 years. It will not, however, have quite "tripled" in that time. But given that it won't be long until it actually did triple (late in that same decade, but prior to this scene), the math is close enough for Tim.

"**At the same time we're using**…" *(p. 20)*
Another example of "things affect other things."

"Be fruitful and multiply" *(p. 21)*
I tend to forget just how controversial this section is: not just for references to sex, but for the inevitable question that it implies: "If this is such a problem, then what are we supposed to do about it?"

The unfortunate combination of global warming and overpopulation is already killing people on a daily basis: whether it is through heat stroke, fire, hurricane or something else, these numbers are trending upwards.

It is, of course, much simpler to suggest that God created that fire/flood/heat wave, just as it is easier to insist that God created that latest billion-people milestone… ignoring that we had a hand in both processes.

And so, once again, we find ourselves bumping our heads on the seemingly immovable ceiling of "God's plan." If every person on the planet, and every leaf on every tree is part of an unknowable ordained strategy for humanity and the Earth, then we will remain ever frozen in our ability to take any action (including those actions aimed at saving humanity and saving the Earth). If scripture (of any denomination) is to be believed, such "plans" seem inconsistent with the compassion and reverence and care that those same scriptures imply with regard to their benevolent deity.

And yet, however much our impulse towards faith may guide us to evacuate that space of understanding and action designated as "God's," the vacuum that our absence creates leaves a space into which other human beings will inevitably enter who *do* have their own such plans. Those who have long made a comfortable living off of releasing carbon into the air will fight to satisfy their addictions to those comforts in the face of all evidence of the damage inflicted on God's creatures and the planet.

And so, at some point, the hard questions about population, energy, and quality of life will need to be asked and answered if we as a race are to survive. As long as it is acceptable for some to insist that "God means for us to suffer and die in the fiery hell of our own making," then that is likely the result that we will manifest.

"Us against the Spotted Owl..." *(p. 21)*
In the early 1990s the Northern Spotted Owl was listed as an endangered species, a designation that brought with it rulings that necessitated the protection of certain old-growth forest areas in the Pacific Northwest. The logging industry claimed that up to 168,000 logging jobs would be lost, while environmentalists argued that protection for the spotted owl has, as a result, protected other threatened species, as well as an entire ecosystem (which, of course, includes humans, too).

[n.b., Even as I write this note, an email rolls in alerting me to a proposed "rollback of the Endangered Species Act."]

"That now is worth nothing..." *(p. 21)*
Money (in this scenario) is now worth nothing. It strikes me that this bears repetition. A lifetime of valuing money leads us to forget that money has no intrinsic value of its own. The only thing that keeps money valuable is our social *agreement* that money is, indeed, of a certain value. Once "society" disintegrates, the value of money disappears (and we wonder why we staked so much of our very existence on the struggle for its acquisition).

"God rolling lower for us..." *(p. 21)*
If you Google "senator with a snowball," you will likely stumble upon an infamous video of an actual US Senator (James Inhofe), arguing on February 26, 2015 that, despite the fact that 2014 had been the hottest year on record (which would quickly be edged out by an even hotter 2016), the fact that it was cold enough outside for him to collect and bring inside, a snowball, then global warming must thereby be "hysteria."

Next, surf for "believe the senator with the snowball" for a vigorous counter-argument from Senator Sheldon Whitehouse.

That same Sen. Inhofe also once said "God's still up there. The arrogance of people to think that we, human beings, would be able to change what he is doing in the climate is to me outrageous." In the absence of agreement, and under the lure of financial remuneration, there will always be insincere actors willing to weaponize God for financial or political advantage.

Commandment Seven: Acknowledge. Screamingly Impossible. Improbabilities. *(p. 22)*
As the planet shows us more evidence of its acceleration towards change, we find ourselves bombarded with news of record temperatures, although we rarely hear that news connected to the phenomenon of Climate Change. The heat wave of July, 2018 (just behind us, as I write this in August) spawned some 127 segments of programming on the major television networks. Only one of those news segments "so much as mentioned climate change." (NYMag.com, July 26, 2018, "How Did the End of the World Become Old News" by David Wallace-Wells)

The current list of the ten hottest years on record lists only one year (1998) that is ***not*** from our current relatively new century. The four "hottest years of all (recorded) time" include 1) 2016, 2) 2015, 3) 2017 and 4) 2014. The anomaly of 2017 falling into 3rd place is thought to be due to the "El Nino" effect of 2014-2016. Or, as Deke Arndt of National Centers for Environmental Information suggested: It's "like riding on an escalator over time..." El Nino "is like jumping up and down" while continuing to ride the escalator upwards. (Wikipedia: "Instrumental temperature record")

"To owls and bees and coral reefs..." *(p. 22)*
Losing bees: "Population levels of more than 700 North American bee species are declining as habitat loss and pesticide use continue at a breakneck pace... Nearly a quarter [of 1400 species monitored] is at risk of extinction." (Time Magazine, "More than 700 Norh American Bee Species are Headed Toward Extinction," Justin Worland, March 2, 2017)

Losing Coral Reefs: "The world's coral reefs, from the Great Barrier Reef neighboring Australia to the Seychelles off the coast of East Africa are in grave danger of dying out completely by mid-century unless carbon emissions are reduced enough to slow ocean warming... and consequences could be severe for millions of people. Coral reefs are known as "the ocean's rainforests," protecting coastlines and providing habitat for "a fourth of the world's fish." (National Geographic, "Coral Reefs Could be Gone in 30 Years," by Laura Parker and Craig Welch, June 23, 2017)

"Tralfamadore…" *(p. 23)*
"Tralfamadore" is a fictional planet from the work of Kurt Vonnegut Jr., mentioned in several of his novels, most notably, "Slaughterhouse Five" and "The Sirens of Titan." (We have assumed, up to this point, that the reader already has a general familiarity with the more familiar science-fictional worlds and beings of "Star Trek," "Star Wars" and "The Lord of the Rings.")

"Corporations Are People, My Friend" *(p. 23)*
Mitt Romney actually said this, amid his run for President in 2012.

What was so striking about Romney's comment was the blithe assurance with which he seemed to assume that everyone would immediately accept this clearly self-contradictory statement. The history of this paradox reaches back to a mostly forgotten "header note" in a Supreme Court decision, and the failure of the Fourteenth Amendment to distinguish between "people" and "natural persons."

The Fourteenth Amendment, adopted in 1868, drawn up with the intent of guaranteeing "equal protection of the laws" to "all persons," was ostensibly intended to protect the rights of African American former slaves, giving them full rights of citizenship. The amendment, however, fails to distinguish between "persons" and "natural persons."

Senator Roscoe Conkling, a former lawyer for the railroads, on the committee writing the Fourteenth Amendment later testified that he "had intentionally inserted the word 'person' instead of the correct legal phrase 'natural person' to describe who would get the protections of the Amendment," thereby keeping the language sufficiently ambiguous as to support later challenges.[15] (Ironically, Fourteenth Amendment cases are brought before the court to challenge issues of corporate law far more often than the racial discrimination issues it was intended to address.)

In numerous cases, corporations have been understood and treated as "artificial persons." And in the 1886 case of Santa Clara County vs. Southern Pacific Railroad, the Supreme Court Justice writing the ruling acknowledged that the court was bypassing any deeper consideration

---

[15] Hartman, Thom, "Unequal Protection: The rise of corporate dominance and theft of human rights," Berrett-Koehler Publishers, Inc., San Francisco, 2010. (Much of this discussion is distilled from "The Theft of Human Rights," posted at thomhartmann.com)

of corporate personhood, but was dealing strictly with the issue of whether the taxes to the railroads regarding "the fences on the line of the railroads should have been valued and assessed."

In publishing this ruling, however, the Court Reporter, J.C. Bancroft Davis, probably under the influence or direction of zealous railroad advocate, Justice Stephen J. Field, wrote "headnotes" describing the context within which the decision was made: "Before argument Mr. Chief Justice Waite said: 'The court does not wish to hear argument on the question whether the provision in the Fourteenth Amendment to the Constitution, which forbids a State to deny to any person within its jurisdiction the equal protection of the laws, applies to these corporations. We are all of the opinion that it does.'"

In other words, the statement that "equal protection under the law" applies to corporations was *not* intended to be part of this minor ruling on tax jurisdiction. If anything, the Chief Justice intended to AVOID discussion of "corporate personhood" while J.C. Bancroft Davis, in his note baldly asserted that the case had been considered in the context of corporate personhood *as an assumed fact.*

This mistaken interpretation of a single Supreme Court ruling has, in turn, imbued corporations with all those rights normally reserved to "persons" under the law. When we add this to later rulings of the court, such as the notion that "money equals speech," we get a cascade of pro-corporate court decisions, such as the insistence that the right of "people" (corporations) to "speak" (through their donations to political causes) cannot be abridged, and in its wake, we find Congress incapable of placing reasonable restrictions on the now-massive influence of money on the U.S. political process.

Add to *that* the notion that (as "Tim" notes), "Corporations must act to maximize profit," and we find ourselves in the thick of a toxic legal brew that sets the planet on a hazardous, possibly fatal, course.

As Thom Hartman quotes William Jennings Bryan, "Man is the handiwork of God and was placed upon earth to carry out a Divine purpose; the corporation is the handiwork of man and created to carry out a money-making policy." (*address to the Ohio 1912 Constitutional Convention*)

Given the Supreme Court's current unwillingness to re-interpret these decisions, the only seeming remedy to this paradox may lie in an amendment to the U.S. Constitution.

"Do unto others..." *(p. 24)*
I include this quote as an obvious reminder to the religious among us that, despite the manner in which climate deniers tend to affiliate themselves with articles of faith, redemption does indeed lie in the words of the words of Jesus, although those particular words are seldom put to use among those looking to turn a profit. (Some form of this rule tends to appear in most religions, to the extent that we rarely attach it to one particular religion in our thinking, citing it, more often than not as "The Golden Rule.")

"Deep down we all knew..." *(p. 24)*
Tim may be exaggerating to suggest that "we all knew." Or, perhaps he is referring to a near-future/more-recent-past in which many of these issues have crystalized for the public-at-large.

But the behavior pattern described is fairly undeniable. No one wants to be the first to relinquish the advantages afforded by modern civilization. (How extremely un-cool do we regard those Luddites without computers or those Quakers in horse-and-buggy?) It would take an act of government intervention to introduce carbon-reducing legislation which would "level the playing field" of restrictions, ensuring that the "pain" of such restrictions would be distributed evenly, in such a way that survival of the race might be possible.

Of course, limitations and restrictions are never popular, and politicians understand that draconian measures might spell and end to their career aspirations. This leaves us traveling in circles, as the anticipated devastation of climate disaster needs to outweigh the immediate suffering of carbon restriction, before we are fully inspired to take any action. In order to reach that "tipping point," does the Earth itself need to go into a spiral of destruction from which no return will be possible?

Or, is it possible to stir into the imagination of the public such awareness of the looming consequences that they would be ready to welcome such draconian measures before all is lost?

Or, are we, perhaps, beyond that "tipping point" already?

"We indulge that much more..." *(p. 25)*
As I write this, I would describe us as living in the era of "The Indulgence," and I desperately hope it is just a phase. With a significant minority (roughly 30%) of the public not yet convinced that climate-change is man-made (perhaps, in many cases, fighting the sub-conscious awareness of its truth), there is a certain predictable resistance to change, occasionally manifesting as a defiant, flaunting consumption of carbon, leading some government figures to lift regulation rather than tighten it, and the occasional truck that overtly vomits smoke into the air. (One such toxic nightmare recently passed me on the road with a license plate that spelled out "NOPRIUS".) It strikes me as a last, desperate fling of denial, before the anticipated clampdown of regulation... "giving the finger' to those who would control them or take away their "freedom."

There was a hot second in which I almost named this play "Fait Accompli," if only because it is our hopeless attitude in facing down a seeming *fait accompli* that is, perhaps, half of the problem. And then I realized that people might assume from the title that I was intending to underline the hopelessness of it all... which is ***not*** my intended goal.

"Which is easy for me here to say..." *(p. 25)*
Of course, I couldn't leave "Tim" as some kind of superior do-gooder who, quite literally, delivers his commandments from on high, as some model of perfection. Who could believe, accept or follow such a smug jerk? It is, rather, the *imperfect* jerks with whom we may identify and hope to follow.

Of course, Tim has offered hints of imperfections throughout, but up until now, we may have simply seen that as false humility.

In my mind, "Tim" has always been me, and the closest I come to acknowledging that is my reference to "kept on with driving my route." As an actor performing one-man plays in the U.S. and Canada, I have spent the better part of the past sixteen years on the road, driving over 700,000 miles, pumping my own "ton of carbon" into the air. I am every bit as guilty of this as each of you who might read this. I like to console myself with the assurance that those people at the receiving end of my efforts have grown in knowledge and awareness, and, on some rare occasions, my guilt has led me to donate to "carbon offsets," contributing to the planting of trees or the restoration of wetlands.

With this play, I have been forced, like Tim, to acknowledge the "carbon on my own hands." I expect that anyone who ever plays this role (assuming anyone else ever will) will ultimately face down the same realization.

There was an earlier draft of this play in which Tim was actually some kind of a traveling solar-panel/air-conditioning salesman, in which he internally justified his travels by replacing carbon-burning systems with renewable energy, but it all got a little silly as I found him providing elaborate justifications in reference to a profession that I knew absolutely nothing about. I found myself gradually cutting this or that reference, until I found that the best solution was to not send the play chasing down this rabbit hole to begin with.

As best we know, Tim is somebody who travels in his line of work, had an imaginative and, coincidentally, accurate vision about the approaching end-game, and some unexplained ability in the realm of construction and installation (or, perhaps, enough money to hire folks with those abilities).

Yes, in the long run, this doesn't all quite match up and make sense as a consistent character or personality.

But, you know: poetic license. Tim is a creation of theatrical art, and needs to live as a kind of "everyman," if only so the audience can see themselves in his thoughts and his choices. (Which seems to be the reaction this play has been getting.)

"And hoped no one would notice..." *(p. 26)*
Tim, here, recreates the moment of realization that all his efforts overlooked one tiny but crucial flaw: This situation is likely to draw attention to itself. We may assume that the door is sufficiently sealed for protection, but the solar panels and the air conditioning unit are exposed outside. It is, perhaps, pure luck that the people outside did not respond violently to the exposed equipment of the covetous "miser" who had locked himself within.

"Yes, it is competition..." *(p. 27)*
Tim is obviously guilty of his own most searing indictment of those "others" he would otherwise lecture.

"But maybe you get ahead of the curve..." *(p. 27)*
Of course, it is the audience who is the "you" who has, perhaps, one last opportunity to get ahead of the curve, which is, more or less, the point of all science fiction. The choice to make any adjustment to their behavior now belongs to them.

To facilitate that possibility, I made a list of the "Ten Commandments" that came up through the course of the play, and make that available to the audience as a program that could be passed out/posted/made available as they exit the building. I'll add that to the end of this commentary.

"Record this and send it ahead..." *(p. 28)*
In acknowledgement of the fact that I do, indeed, "steal from the best," this impulse of Tim's to "record this and send it ahead" is a little bit of a nod to "Hamlet," who, dying, begs Horatio, "If thou didst ever hold me in thy heart, absent thee from felicity awhile. And in this harsh world draw thy breath in pain to tell my story."

I didn't write this passage thinking that I was copying Hamlet. But when I got it down on paper, and stepped back to look at it, I realized just how universal this impulse is: we all want to send messages to the world (or, in this case, the universe) from beyond the grave... if only to live the slightest trace beyond the edges of our limited mortal being, in the hearts and minds of a someone or someones left behind.

"2028" (Ten years ahead) *(p. 28)*
I have withheld this crucial piece of information until this moment. Most likely you, the audience, have accumulated enough evidence by now that you know this is not happening in the oft-predicted 50-100-year time span. Tim knows too much about contemporaneous 2018 political figures (and expresses zero references to events/figures of a distant future).

It is also a somewhat self-evident device for Tim to cite the precise date, precisely ten years into the future. That final phrase of this play has clearly been manipulated to send a message to you, the audience, sitting here today: "tick-tock."

It is also a self-conscious acknowledgement that this is not (and cannot be) 100% "real." I am taking/have taken a poetic license, and have no way of knowing if this is the fate that awaits us. Also "Tim" and his exploits are a larger-than-life situation we find ourselves living into. Tim sometimes expresses himself with an extreme facility for improvised poetic trope, because it is all written down by some unknown, unseeable hand who has thought out these thoughts and organized them into something meaningful.

And now it is up to us to grasp, however well that we might, at that meaning, and to make some greater sense of the world and what we might want to do with it over the ten years to come.

The Commandments[16]

1) Whatever planet you live on, you evolved without air conditioning. Your planet is *by definition, habitable*. Work with it.

2) Stop idling.

3) Do not get too attached to any given technology. Just because you CAN do it, and MIGHT use it, doesn't mean you OUGHT to.

4) The cost of buying a thing needs to reflect the expense it inflicts on the planet, at large.

5) Those who set up your laws must not profit therein.

6) Don't get over your skis. Grow only to where you can sustain the thread.

7) Acknowledge. Screamingly impossible. Improbabilities.

8) Each one arrives.

9) "Robots can't consciously injure a human, or through some inaction allow that a human might so come to harm." (Isaac Asimov, *First Law of Robotics*)

10) If the best I might offer is but one more day to the next generation, then I owe them that day, or that hour, that minute.

11) Which is easy for me, here, to say.

---

16 *I know: WAY PRETENTIOUS for me to list these out! Calling them "commandments" may just be my way of offering several discrete thoughts and prioritizing. I'm sharing them just in case there's that one ore two that struck you as important, and you can't remember what it was.*

Also available from TMRT Press…! And on tour…!

Breakneck Hamlet!

★ ★ ★ ★ ★ [There's an] 'I can't believe he's really going to do this' feel... If you're a fan of Shakespeare, it's a must see… a highly entertaining experience that's worth the price of admission. *David Martin Botwick-Ries, Vue Weekly*

★ ★ ★ ★ **1/2** Mooney has done every time-stressed fan of the doubting Dane a great service… a great introduction. *Gordon Kent, Edmonton Journal*

The buzz… was so enthusiastic I headed down to see what all the fuss was about… Tim had the audience in stiches. *Louis B. Hobson, Calgary Herald.*

Breathes fresh life and excitement into the epic tale… energetic and riveting… He leaps between the various players in a single breath, all the time rushing towards the final and bloody end… must see theatre. *James Hutchison, jameshutchison.ca*

Madcap, high-energy… This is the way Shakespeare should be taught… Mooney brings it together with tremendous passion and way more energy than any one man ought to possess. *Allison Carter, IndyStar.com*

[The recurring themes] are lit up in neon lights… a whirlwind of wonderful. Hold on to your seats and watch a master at his work. *Lee Hartman, KCMetropolis.org*

Must See: What an hour it is!... *Breakneck Hamlet* is truly breakneck, and may leave you panting with exertion. *Maren Longbella, Twin Cities Pioneer Press*

Brilliant… [Mooney] seamlessly throws in asides, explanations and famous lines as he whirls to the play's conclusion. *Jodie Jacobs, Examiner.com*

Astonishing… a concise cliff-hanger... Gestures are precise, elaborate and underlined by stark changes in vocal tone… an assured and lively adaptation. *Jay Harvey, jayharveyupstage.blogspot.com*

It runs rings around that other performance by Mel Gibson. *Dan Grossman, Nuvo*

Yes, it is all the best of this best of all plays. *Debra Ann Christensen*

Luminous linguistic beauty… theatrically accessible, remarkably clear, and vibrantly alive. *Robert Hubbard*

Tim's asides be mirthful yet unforced; his energy like a monsoon; his acting clear & stellar; & best of all, his unique narration doth illuminate the story such that even I—Hamlet-soaked for nigh 3 decades—didst see things I had not seen afore now, & I LEARNED ANEW. The rest is silence. *Amy Salloway*

Breakneck Julius Caesar!

Five Stars: This performance needs to be filmed and sold to school districts nationwide… interesting and compelling… Mooney races through the piece with accuracy and sweat. He's well-prepared, focused, and magnificent in his performance. *Bob Evans, KC Applauds*

Remarkably cogent… always excellent… His preparation and rehearsal are obvious, seamless and audience-appreciated. *Alan Portner, Broadway World*

Mooney is like the high-school English teacher you always wished you had… His elocution is so well-enunciated that it illuminates the archaic language for the modern ear… Best of all are Mooney's snarky asides, fourth-wall-shattering footnotes that poke fun at the play's oddities… Even if you usually fall asleep during sword-and-sandal sagas, lend Mooney your ears for this hour of electrifying edutainment. *Seth Kubersky, Orlando Weekly*

Fasten your seat belts… 60 cardiovascular minutes that leave Mooney sweating, and his audience shouting 'Huzzah!'… The perfect guide for this Elizabethan journey, which is enjoyable for "literary-dorks" and "Shakespeare-virgins" alike… like mixing your Shakespearean Sparknotes with a triple shot of espresso. *Lania Berger, Orlando Sentinel*

Yet another outstanding production… The Shakespeare tragedy has never been so much fun and simultaneously instructive. It's a Fringe go-to…
Deborah Hirsch, The Pitch

So great… a one man display of dramatic prowess, with real time commentary that criticizes the story's details through a modern lens… a Shakespeare production that's well worth seeing. *Kevin Pennyfeather, Vue Weekly*

It's all amazing stuff… Mooney's seamless editing of the Bard means that he's kept all the good stuff… [with] a fresh interpretation of Brutus… that changes the whole texture of the play methinks. Hey, I'm convinced. Huzzah!
Marc Horton, 12th night.ca

A feat of condensation and memorization with humor… an outstanding performance. *Todd James, Global News Canada*

I never ceased to be impressed and delighted by Mooney's virtuosic performance… What's left is for the audience to hold on to their seats and resist blinking for the next 60 minutes… a must see—a theatrical treat, really.
Hephzibah Dutt, KC Fringe Reviewer

Shakespeare's Histories

Ten Epic Plays at a Breakneck Pace!

Dazzling, robust, dedicated, and nothing short of brilliant artistry… comparable to Carl Sagan's interpretation of the Cosmos. Only faster, and funnier.
Eduardo Santiago, Award-winning Author of "Midnight Rumba"

A slim volume of clear, accessible explanations of the history behind Shakespeare's plays. A dizzying performance text… This is the most fun you'll ever have preparing for *Richard III*. *Eileen Polk, The Tudor Guild*

The implications for lesson plans and cross-disciplines of drama, speech, and English are limitless… For the novice performer or the well-informed scholar, a must-read/must-own addition.
Aaron Adair, PhD, Assistant Dean, Southeastern Oklahoma University

An absolutely wonderful new approach… I will be incorporating this in any Shakespeare or Dramatic Literature class I'll be teaching… a delight even to those already familiar. *Melissa Berry, Mount St. Mary's College, Los Angeles*

Mooney connects the dots... a staggering amount of material—war, murder, deception, banishment, conquests, family drama, and much more. Mooney makes it accessible, enjoyable, and fun. *Kristin Shafel Omiccioli, KCMetropolis.org*

Colorful and concise… leaving you entertained and feeling smarter.
Liz Cook & Deborah Hirsch, The Pitch.com

The great, grand picture of the wars of English succession will fill itself in your mind more complete than ever… a quick jump-start in a lifelong love of some of the greatest plays ever written. *Kelly Luck, KCStage.com*

Spookily impressive… a torrent of knowledge… A do-not-miss show…
Jessica Bryce Young, Orlando Weekly

If only cramming for an exam were as enjoyable... It's an epic in an hour… It's best when the exhaustingly energetic Mooney introduces you to rich, complex characters like the existentially conflicted Richard II or Joan of Arc as seen through Elizabethan eyes (the little witch). Mooney brings welcome clarity to what all those wars and words were about. *Rob Hubbard, Pioneer Press*

An awesome thing to see, in the sense that it will fill you with awe — awe that one person can remember all those Shakespearean speeches, the different mannerisms and voices for each character, and make it all interesting… Mooney makes sharp, witty insights into Shakespeare's choices [and] truly brings the stories to life.
Liz Byron, Aisle Say Twin Cities

Molière Than Thou

Best of Fringe: Best Adapted Work. *San Francisco Fringe Festival*

The audience is enthralled… Timothy Mooney is the real deal… A very tight performance indeed, which should be seen by any aspiring actor who wants to tread the boards. *George Psillidies, nytheatre.com*

"Top Ten of 2006" One-of-a-kind… original, weird and seriously funny… one of the most creative and refreshing pieces of classical theatre I've seen in years… Mooney's translations make Molière's 17th century language instantly accessible. His interpretations were crisp, stylized and sang with the comic genius of the playwright's original intent. *Ruth Cartlidge, Chattanooga Pulse*

Mooney is clearly enraptured by the great French playwright… The translations are wonderful… well worth seeing. *Amy Barratt, Montreal Mirror*

The humanities are in safe hands this year. *San Francisco Bay Guardian*

Molière has never been more accessible… *Marie J. Kilker, aislesay.com*

Outstanding... A number of patrons found the performance too short, because they could have listened to Mr. Mooney all day. *Ken Gordon, CBC*

The listener can draw all the available pleasure from the splendid speeches penned by the French Shakespeare. *Kevin Prokosh, Winnipeg Free Press*

Clearly Molière lives. *Elizabeth Maupin, Orlando Sentinel*

A must-see for aspiring drama students and a pleasant experience for the rest of us… *The Vue Weekly, Edmonton*

I highly recommend his skilled impersonation of one of the theater's most gifted and important creative spirits. *Al Krulik, Orlando Weekly*

If you're not passionate about Molière now, you may well be at the end of the show… *Marianne Hales Harding, Seattle Fringe Fest Review Rag*

One of the reasons that Molière's work has survived is that, sadly, his enemies have outlived him… But what he left us were his vast quantity of words… articulate, brilliant, hilarious, disgusting, despairing… We need his voice. And he's funny as hell. *Minnesota Fringe Blogger, Phillip Low*

CRITERIA
A ONE-MAN, COMIC, SCI-FI THRILLER!

An engaging and brilliant performance. *Edmonton VueWeekly*

Provocative, funny, thoughtful, shocking and compelling. Stuff like this is what the fringe is all about. See it. *Quentin Mills-Fenn, Winnipeg Uptown*

A sci-fi action flick, a thriller, a mystery and a road movie [with] a riveting edge-of-your-seat finale. *Cheryl Binning, Winnipeg Free Press*

The terrorist enters a diner where His shock and horror at the decadence of a society where a waitress calls everyone "honey" almost brought the house down... *Stacy Rowland, TheatreSeattle.com*

It approaches politics more successfully than any other show... It's smart, it's nuanced – and everybody needs to see it... *Phillip Low, Fringe Blogger*

Along with his signature comedic timing and vigorous delivery, Timothy Mooney is nothing short of an indefatigable creative force… His flair for storytelling and imaginative worldbuilding completely immersed me in this vision of future America, focusing on totalitarianism, identity, security, and class structure. *Kristin Shafel Omiccioli, KCMetropolis*

…Should be performed for corporate executives or at political gatherings and then discussed all night. *George Savage, Playwright (On-line Review)*

"**One Man Apocalypse**!" "There's not a lot of optimism (though there's plenty of apocalypse-relieving comedy). *Courtney McLean (On-line Review)*

The language in this play is astonishing… pulling us along, off-balance and breathless with incomprehension… If I laughed, it would have to have been the laugh of catastrophe: giddy with hopelessness... a really exciting evening of virtuoso theater. *Richard Greene, Georgia College & State University*

A comic espionage sequence Woody Allen might have written. The drama unfolds at a captivating pace and the dark comedy crackles.
Fringe Review Rag, Seattle 2003

The action is exciting, the consequences chilling and the story telling superb.
Carl Gauze, Ink 19

Very compelling… Hard to explain but easy to enjoy.
Bret Fetzer, The Stranger Weekly Magazine

The Big Book of Molière Monologues

Hilarious Performance Pieces From Our Greatest Comic Playwright

Molière's lines, penned in Classical French over three centuries ago found exuberant reaffirmation in Tim's smooth and stylish English translation... His book of monologues is a masterwork. I've never seen a better compilation.
William Luce, Author, The Belle of Amherst, Barrymore, The Last Flapper

Offers more than the title would suggest. True, there are 160 or so of Molière monologues... But he also provides plot summaries and contextual information, as well as an introduction to the life and work of Molière, guides to the performance of classical verse monologues and stopwatch timings of each piece for audition purposes. *Stage Directions Magazine*

A must-read for Molière's fans and neophytes... a riveting introduction to Molière and his work... incredibly faithful to the spirit of the plays. Mooney was able to put into verse even those works that had been originally written in prose and the effect is outstanding. *Pascale-Anne Brault, DePaul University*

Mooney's exhaustive research, scholarship, and experience has made him one of the world's leading experts on Molière... invaluable to anyone interested in the "nuts and bolts" of 17th century French Comedy... My best advice: buy this book and then bring Mr. Mooney to your institution or venue to see him bring the book to life! *Aaron Adair, Southeastern Oklahoma State University*

FANTASTIC! As an educator, reading it was akin to attending a master class. As a director, I am "chomping at the bit" to work on a Molière piece again.
James McDonnell, Fine Arts Chair, College of the Sequoias

The perfect accompaniment to my study of Molière - a fabulous collection of some of Molière's most hilarious pieces written creatively for the current actor... This book can help you find the perfect monologue before you go searching through every single play out there. *Sean B. (On-Line Review)*

An elegantly simplistic highway of understanding, from the basic description of iambs to the laughed out loud at, skillfully constructed verse... Tim's *Big Book* facilitates this in a very American, in your face way, like Mad Magazine or the old Saturday Night Live... You will be delighted, fulfilled and even a bit smarter in the timeless clever ingenuity of Molière and Mooney's genius manner of bringing this genre to life! *John Paul Molière, Hume, Virginia*

Acting at the Speed of Life;

Conquering Theatrical Style

A unique, refreshing and highly practical approach… No nonsense steps to approach the demands of stylized acting… This exceedingly valuable book will inspire actors to approach stylized theatre with the spirit of fun and style.
James Fisher, Theatre Library Association's "Broadside"

Author Timothy Mooney takes on the challenges of asides, soliloquies and rhetorical speech. He offers tips on memorizing lines, incorporating the "stuff" of historical style, and going beyond naturalism and realism as it suits the playwright's intent. Nicely done. *Stage Directions Magazine*

A gem of a book that demystifies the acting process by mixing common-sense instruction with practical exercises. It ought to have a place on every actor's and director's bookshelf... Keep it handy for audition preparation, classroom studies, rehearsals and sometimes simply for a good read… He inspires his readers with a clear common-sense approach, eye-opening analyses of familiar texts, and wise advice that encourages newcomers and veteran actors to grow into the best they can be. *Michael Howley, Southern Theatre*

Terrific… Replete with incisive, clear-headed accessible advice… The clearest and most comprehensive work for the community and student actor written today. *Dr. Christian H. Moe, Southern Illinois University*

Not just your average acting book: A comprehensive understanding of the basic skills needed to survive. Powerful and empowering… it's necessary for every serious actor's shelf. *Dennis Wemm, Glenville State College*

The hardest-working book in my life of teaching acting to high school students... From the basics of memorization to the clearing of the cobwebs surrounding the classics, the book does it all with grace and great humor.
Claudia Haas, Playwright for Youth/Artist in Residence, Twin Cities

A thunderous success! My cabaret class came alive with interpretive freedom. *Loren F. Salter, Artistic Director and Performance Coach*

Probably the most accessible approach to classical style that I have ever seen.
Celi Oliveto, Master of Letters/MFA Candidate, Mary Baldwin College

This could be the modern manual for the Director and the Actor.
Charley Ault, Director, Players Guild of the Festival Playhouse

NO other book I've read captures these simple tasks that are so important.
Janice Fronczak, University of Nebraska-Kearney